To Nor
Love
Donna Wampler

2 Thess. 3:16

Devotions for Caregivers
and Other Hurting People

By
Donna Buck Wampler

authorHOUSE®

AuthorHouse™
1663 Liberty Drive
Bloomington, IN 47403
www.authorhouse.com
Phone: 1-800-839-8640

© *2010 Donna Buck Wampler. All rights reserved.*

No part of this book may be reproduced, stored in a retrieval system, or transmitted by any means without the written permission of the author.

First published by AuthorHouse 12/10/2010

ISBN: 978-1-4567-1115-3 (sc)
ISBN: 978-1-4567-1116-0 (e)

Printed in the United States of America

Any people depicted in stock imagery provided by Thinkstock are models, and such images are being used for illustrative purposes only. Certain stock imagery © Thinkstock.

This book is printed on acid-free paper.

Scripture, unless otherwise marked, is taken from the HOLY BIBLE, NEW INTERNATIONAL VERSION®. Copyright © 1973, 1978, 1984 Biblica. Used by permission of Zondervan. All rights reserved.

Because of the dynamic nature of the Internet, any Web addresses or links contained in this book may have changed since publication and may no longer be valid. The views expressed in this work are solely those of the author and do not necessarily reflect the views of the publisher, and the publisher hereby disclaims any responsibility for them.

DEDICATION

This book is dedicated to my dear friend Mimi and to our special brother-in-law, Ed, and to all my persevering friends who are serving loved ones. They have been a testimony to God's grace under the extreme pressure of long term caregiving. And it is dedicated to you, gentle reader, as you faithfully carry on. May God bless you all!

ACKNOWLEDGEMENTS

I am first of all grateful to the Lord Jesus Christ who has made me one of His own. I am thankful to my first Bible study leader who, though I had been a believer for many years, introduced me to the joy and power of the Scriptures. I have been blessed by the faithful prayer warriors who have covered the writing of these devotions, and by my precious sister, Suzanne, who proof read and edited.

I am especially thankful for my husband, Joe, without whose support this book would have been impossible.

How do you see God using these verses and these thoughts in your life today?

HOPE IN ANGUISH

2 Be merciful to me, LORD, for I am faint; O LORD, heal me, for my bones are in agony. 3 My soul is in anguish. How long, O LORD, how long? 4 Turn, O LORD, and deliver me; save me because of your unfailing love. …6 I am worn out from groaning; all night long I flood my bed with weeping and drench my couch with tears. 7 My eyes grow weak with sorrow; … for the LORD has heard my weeping. 9 The LORD has heard my cry for mercy; the LORD accepts my prayer. Ps 6:2-9

I have a dear young friend who lost her father. She was devastated. While she was grieving she received many encouraging Scriptures from friends, and they were helpful. Then she candidly asked, "Are there any verses that just express the pain and grief I am feeling?" She wanted to see that others of faith had felt just the same anguish she was feeling. In essence, she wanted someone to cry with her. That is a great part of the value of this passage. We can step into the deep despair of the author and know that we are not alone. Someone else has felt this kind of pain.

Of course there is a second value here, that of assurance. Not only does God hear my weeping, but He has accepted my prayer and mercy is on the way! God is aware and His love will ultimately save us and restore us. He has not, nor will He ever, forsake us. Hear His promise in 1 Peter 5:10:

And the God of all grace, who called you to his eternal glory in Christ, after you have suffered a little while, will himself restore you and make you strong, firm and steadfast.

Prayer

Father, we cry out to you in our grief and anguish. Thank you for hearing our weeping and thank you for accepting our prayers. Help us to remember that at the right time you will lift us from the pit of despair with your own loving hands. Amen

How do you see God using these verses and these thoughts in your life today?

GOD -- LIGHT IN THE DARK TIMES

11 If I say, "Surely the darkness will hide me
and the light become night around me,"
12 even the darkness will not be dark to you;
the night will shine like the day,
for darkness is as light to you. Ps 139:11-12

When I was a youngster my mother sent me to the neighborhood grocery store, a short walk from home. I had done it before and relished the responsibility. But this time it was a bit late in the day and I lingered just a little too long. By the time I started home it was dark! I must have taken a wrong turn as I left the store, for suddenly I didn't know where I was or which way to go and panic set in. Thankfully, a teenage boy who had delivered our paper recognized me, saw my situation and took me safely home.

But the feeling I had then was much like the feeling I have had as an adult when life has seemed to drop me into deep darkness. Panic! Which way should I go? Where will I find the safety I had before? The power of these verses comes as we visualize the God of light in whom there is no darkness. God can see in the dark as though it were not dark, because He is light. He can see right through the darkness that enters our lives because the darkness is not dark to Him. The road to our refuge is always clearly visible to Him no matter how dark it seems to us. If we just take His hand and trust His leading He will, like my teenage rescuer, take us to a place of light and safety. And if we look at Him hard enough and long enough, we may even find the darkness lifting so that we ourselves can begin to see the way.

28 You, O LORD, keep my lamp burning;
my God turns my darkness into light. Ps 18:28

Prayer

Dearest Father, Your very first act of creation was to bring light into the dark chaos that existed where the world was to be. And you are still bringing light into chaotic darkness today. I ask you, I implore you, shine your light into the darkness of my life and show me the way. In Christ who is the Light. Amen.

How do you see God using these verses and these thoughts in your life today?

HIGHER WAYS!

**8 "For my thoughts are not your thoughts, neither
are your ways my ways," declares the LORD.
9 "As the heavens are higher than the earth, so are my ways higher
than your ways and my thoughts than your thoughts. Isa 55:8-9**

When I was a senior in high school one of the highlights of the day was to hang out after school in the local drugstore, drinking cokes and flirting with the boys. My parents were not high on this pastime and one day they insisted that I come right home after school. I was irate -- missing all that fun. But I was also obedient. Yet I got home to find that several of their good friends had dropped by. I could see no good reason for me to be there, too. More irate! I marched sourly to my room to pout. Then my dad called me down. He took me out to the garage. The reason I had to come home, and the reason the friends were there to watch, is because he had bought me a brand new car for my very own! Tears streamed down my face, and of course all thought they were tears of joy. They were not! They were tears of remorse for the unwarranted anger I had felt. His plans for me were so much higher than the plans I had for myself.

So much like my experience, only on a much higher plane, is our heavenly Father's plan for us. We can be angry and untrusting at what we see -- and aren't we so often that way? Yet He tells us ahead of time, "I have a higher, better plan even if you can't see it now."

I saw rather quickly my father's wonderful plan for me, but sometimes we must wait days, years or even a lifetime to understand the better plan God has for us. One day, for sure, (remember, He promised!) we will see it and weep with remorse for our doubt and also rejoice with Him that it has finally been fulfilled.

This passage is followed by a promise:

You will go out in joy and be led forth in peace; Isa 55:12

Hold on to that thought, dear one! His plan will come to fruition.

Prayer

Dear Father, I read that your thoughts are so much higher than any I could have and I believe that's true. However, when things are especially difficult down here, I sometimes have a hard time remembering that truth and I need to pray, "Help Thou my unbelief." Please help me to remember there is a whole dimension that I can't see or even imagine, and you are in charge of it and it is GOOD. Hear my plea, dear Father, in the name of your Son. Amen

How do you see God using these verses and these thoughts in your life today?

DEPENDING ON THE ROCK

5 Find rest, O my soul, in God alone; my hope comes from him. 6 He alone is my rock and my salvation; he is my fortress, I will not be shaken. 7 My salvation and my honor depend on God; he is my mighty rock, my refuge. 8 Trust in him at all times, O people; pour out your hearts to him, for God is our refuge. Ps 62:5-8

When life gets tough we all look for a place of safety -- a shelter from the storm that assails us. We look to doctors, and doctors are good. We look to friends, and friends are helpful. We look to family, and family is wonderful. But sometimes none of these is enough. Our burden is so heavy that it locks us in an isolated place where no one can understand or help. It seems there are no answers.

But God can reach us there! In the words of this Psalm He offers exactly what we need most - a secure place. He alone is our rock, our fortress, our refuge. He alone is the source of our hope, and in Him alone can we ultimately find the rest we cry out for.

How do we find this mighty sanctuary? He tells us two steps to take. We trust in Him at all times and then we must pour out our hearts to Him. We must tell Him our heaviness, tell Him our pain. He hears and He comes, and He cradles us safely in His everlasting arms. O what a blessed place of comfort!

PRAYER

Dear Lord, I feel like my world is coming apart. Please help me find that place of peace and rest -- the security of trusting everything and everyone in my life to you. Amen

How do you see God using these verses and these thoughts in your life today?

SEPARATION

16 But Ruth replied, "Don't urge me to leave you or to turn back from you. Where you go I will go, and where you stay I will stay. Your people will be my people and your God my God. 17 Where you die I will die, and there I will be buried. May the LORD deal with me, be it ever so severely, if anything but death separates you and me." 18 When Naomi realized that Ruth was determined to go with her, she stopped urging her. Ruth 1:16-17

`My mother was dying! Though she was almost in a coma she fluttered her eyes from time to time with occasional flashes of recognition. The day before she died I was holding her hand in the hospital room. Suddenly she opened her eyes and said clearly to me, "I know how much you love me." Not, "I love you," but "I know how much you love me!" With that she fell back into her coma for the last time.

There is no way to express the comfort those words have given me in the years since she died. As I have raised my children, planned my daughter's wedding, cared for new grandchildren, and faced many of life's experiences from a more mature point of view, I have often been surprised by a sense of regret when I remembered times of not understanding or fully appreciating all Mom had done for me. It was too late to say thanks, or to apologize where necessary, but whenever those feeling came I recalled her final words to me and found great comfort. She knew! My mother knew that in spite of my mistakes or omissions I had loved her! And knowing she knew was enough.

Most difficult when we lose connection (through death, sickness, or physical separation) with those who are precious to us is the inability to reaffirm our mutual love. 1 Corinthians 13:7-8 tell us that love **" bears all things, believes all things, hopes all things, endures all things. Love never fails."** (NKJV) It remains when the connection is gone. Dear one, rely on the memories that reaffirm that love. Let them be strong enough to combat the moments of loneliness or regret. **"And now abide faith, hope, love, these three; but the greatest of these is love. (1 Cor 13:13 NKJV)**

Prayer

Lord God, will you help me to both give and receive love even when all physical connection is gone. May my joyful memories confirm the love we had and help me release regrets and grief. In the precious name of Jesus, the Source of all love. Amen

How do you see God using these verses and these thoughts in your life today?

GIVE THANKS

**Give thanks to the LORD, for he is good;
his love endures forever. Ps. 118:1**

That is so not an easy thing to do in the midst of the mire of struggle! The first thought that comes to mind is that it might actually be dishonest to give thanks when I don't feel grateful. And yet, our Father commands it over and over in His word. One wonders why. Why is it so important that we are told to **"give thanks in all circumstances, for this is God's will for you in Christ Jesus"? (1 Thess 5:18)**

As alien as this seems in the heart of my hurt I must admit that the times I have remembered and obeyed this command the strangest things have happened in my soul. At first it was just obedience and gradually it became more. It was mind expanding in that I began to imagine that maybe there actually was going to be a good reason or a good outcome -- God might just be up to something -- and my hope began to bloom. Then it was faith expanding as I continued to focus on God in my circumstances. It gave me comfort as I realized that no matter how it turned out He was with me. The same Psalmist wrote just a few lines down in this Psalm,

"5 In my anguish I cried to the LORD, and he answered by setting me free. 6 The LORD is with me; I will not be afraid. What can man do to me? ….13 I was pushed back and about to fall, but the LORD helped me. 14 The LORD is my strength and my song; he has become my salvation.

From these words we know he was not having an easy time either. Yet praising God somehow lifted him to glorious heights in the midst of his pain. God's answer was setting him free. Free from what? Free from the fear of what might be, from the heaviness of being alone, from the prison of hopelessness! He even adds joyous notes to his song, getting stronger in spirit as his praises continues. Read on. "**v.15: Shouts of joy and victory resound in the tents of the righteous: "The LORD's right hand has done mighty things! …24 This is the day the LORD has made; let us rejoice and be glad in it.**

The writer ends on the same note, the same wise council with

which he began. **29 Give thanks to the LORD, for he is good; his love endures forever.**

So while it may take grit as we begin, just maybe when we start to lift our hearts in praise to a Father whose love "endures forever" we will find that hope and comfort. Psalm 22 tells us we will even find the very presence of God Himself, and no matter what else is going on in our lives that will bless and sustain us!

But thou art holy, O thou that inhabitest the praises of Israel. Ps 22:33 (KJV)

Prayer

Oh Holy Father, whose love for us knows no limits, your commands from the beginning have always been for our very own good. Now as you tell us in our worst of times to look up and praise you, we can know it is your best wisdom for our needs. We will find you -- your comfort, hope and very presence, and Lord how we need that! I do praise you from my very heart for offering me this avenue, this bridge to yourself. Thank you, thank you, my Blessed Holy and loving Father. Amen

How do you see God using these verses and these thoughts in your life today?

THERE, I'VE SAID IT AGAIN

3 Set a guard over my mouth, O LORD;
keep watch over the door of my lips. Ps 141:3

Oh, Lord, I've done it again! I've blurted out hurtful words in my frustration. My father used to have a wonderful prayer that makes more and more sense to me the longer I live. It was, "Dear Lord, make my words sweet and tender for tomorrow I may have to eat them". Why can't I remember that?

When we are weighed down with problems and fears it is so easy to just boil over and lash out at the very people we love the most. Then, of course, we are overcome with guilt and remorse. What are we to do? Well, Jesus died for our guilt to be released and He lives to give us the power to control our words. David found the answer and so did Job. They lashed out in their deep frustration and pain, but they lashed out at the very one who could handle it --the One who, I think, even welcomed and honored their honesty. Only God loves us enough to accept our outbursts, is wise enough to understand why we feel that way and is powerful enough to give us release and healing.

The very fact that He put this prayer in His holy Scriptures lets us know that He understands our needs for 'mouth control' and He shows us what to do about it -- turn to the One who made our mouths and ask for help.

. Ps 18:6 In my distress I called to the LORD; I cried
to my God for help. From his temple he heard my
voice; my cry came before him, into his ears.

Prayer

Father, forgive me. I have lost control again. Thank you that you understand, you forgive and you even help my loved ones to forgive me. Now I ask you, I plead with you, "Set a guard over my mouth, O Lord; keep watch over the door to my lips." In the name of my understanding Savior. Amen.

How do you see God using these verses and these thoughts in your life today?

HIS WORD IS TRUE!

**5 Trust in the LORD with all your heart
and lean not on your own understanding;
6 in all your ways acknowledge him,
and he will make your paths straight. Prov 3:5-6**

When I was ten years old our family made our first trip to Florida. One evening while we were strolling down the street from our hotel, we passed a shop that said "Yacht Broker" on the window.

"Daddy," I asked, "What is a 'ya-chet'?

"Honey, that's pronounced 'yacht', and it's a big boat," he replied.

Well, the word looked like 'ya-chet' to me, but for all the rest of my life I have known it says 'yacht' because no matter what it looked like, I had my father's word on it.

That is essentially what God is saying to us in these verses. "Things are not always what they may seem, but take My word for it -- don't lean on your own understanding." God means what He says and He says He is still and always directing our steps.

PRAYER

Father, Help me to trust you, to believe your word even if it doesn't seem to make sense to me. If you say it, it must be true. And thank you for your promise to direct my every step when I acknowledge you. Amen

How do you see God using these verses and these thoughts in your life today?

PATIENCE

7 Be still before the LORD and wait patiently for him; Ps 37:7

I waited patiently for the LORD; he turned to me and heard my cry. 2 He lifted me out of the slimy pit, out of the mud and mire; he set my feet on a rock and gave me a firm place to stand. 3 He put a new song in my mouth, a hymn of praise to our God. Many will see and fear and put their trust in the LORD. Ps 40:1-3

13 I am still confident of this: I will see the goodness of the LORD in the land of the living. 14 Wait for the LORD; be strong and take heart and wait for the LORD. Ps 27:13-14

Waiting! It is not easy. But what makes it a little less difficult, usually, is our sense of expectation. We wait for a bus and we expect it will come in "x" number of minutes. We wait for a baby and we know it will be born in a certain number of months. We wait for special times and we can count the days as they pass, one by one, until the anticipated day arrives. But when it comes to waiting for the Lord, we seem to lose that sense of expectation. Despair slips in uninvited and shoves us into the "slimy pit." "Where is God?" we ask. "Is He really going to come to me?" "Will He ever make a difference?"

These verses remind us that when our waiting is over we will sing a new song; we will stand on solid rock. We can expect God to be there! I have been told that Psalm 27:13 has been translated, **"I would have despaired if I had not expected to see the goodness of the Lord in the land of the living."**

When we truly begin to expect to see Him at the end of our waiting, our despair will begin to blossom into hope, and that hope grow into confidence and strength.

Prayer

My Father and my God, Help me to expect to find you at the end of my waiting, and may that expectation color all my days of waiting with hope, confidence and strength. Amen

How do you see God using these verses and these thoughts in your life today?

THE KEY TO PEACE

**3 You will keep in perfect peace him whose mind
is steadfast, because he trusts in you.
4 Trust in the LORD forever, for the LORD, the
LORD, is the Rock eternal. Isa 26:3-4**

I learned the power of these verses when I was diagnosed with breast cancer. In the first few hours I felt like my world was ending, and my imagination ran wild. I attended my own funeral over and over in my mind, and continued to mentally live out my final hours. Then this verse came to me. "Stop the negative thoughts," it cried to me! "Look beyond the diagnosis and keep your eyes on God!"

God is an eternal Rock and nothing that enters our lives can change that. I began to set my mind on Him and truly, He kept His promise as stated here. He kept me in such a perfect peace that it has been settled in my mind forever, He is able to be trusted. Dear one, set your focus on Him and He will give you peace!

Prayer

Dearest Father, our Rock eternal, you know our desperate cry for peace in this difficult world, and in this difficult situation. You knew we would need it and you planned in eternity past to provide that for each of your children. In these verses you have given us a roadmap to the place where that peace abounds. Help us turn our gaze upon you, looking past our fears and sorrows, and then, Father, fill our aching hearts with your supernatural peace. Thank you for understanding our need and showing us the path to peace. Amen

How do you see God using these verses and these thoughts in your life today?

DIRECT YOUR "WHY'S" TO HIM

**9 I say to God my Rock, "Why have you forgotten me?
Why must I go about mourning, oppressed by the enemy?" 10
My bones suffer mortal agony as my foes taunt me, saying to me
all day long, "Where is your God?" 11 Why are you downcast,
O my soul? Why so disturbed within me? Put your hope in God,
for I will yet praise him, my Savior and my God. Ps 42:9-11**

My dear neighbor lost her son tragically in an automobile accident. Her first word to me was "Why?"

Surely she is not the only one who has asked this question. You, yourself, may well be asking it right now. And perhaps you even feel a little guilty for asking it. Is it sinful, we wonder; is it all right to be mad at God? Can we raise a fist and ask, "Where are you?" "Why are you doing this to me?"

As we read this Psalm we can know that we are not the only ones who do that! In fact, I think this passage is telling us that God is the very Person to whom we should direct our questions. Truly He is the only one who has any kind of answer at all. And He knows if our pain and anger turn us to Him, even if it is to ask why, we are at the same time turning to the answer. **"Put your hope in God, for I will yet praise him, my Savior and my God."** This is the answer for every downcast soul who is screaming questions of doubt to the Father. He doesn't say how and He doesn't say when, but He promises He will again show us Himself, and we will yet praise Him.

Prayer

Where are you, my God? My soul is in anguish and I cannot find help! Ah, but Abba Father, Daddy, you know my grief. You anguished over the death of your beloved Son so that I could have hope when my days of anguish came. Thank you for your intimate identification with me, and for the tiny flickers of hope that begin to blossom in my heart when I come to you. In the name of your Beloved One. Amen

How do you see God using these verses and these thoughts in your life today?

HE KNOWS!

**"For the LORD your God has blessed you in all the work
of your hand. He knows your trudging through this great
wilderness. These forty years the LORD your God has been
with you; you have lacked nothing.'" Deut 2:7 (NKJV)**

Just before the Israelites were about to enter the Promised Land, Moses summed up the highlights of their forty year journey from Egypt through the wilderness. Early in his remembrance these words jump out. **"He knows your trudging through this great wilderness."**

It's true for you as well. The Lord knows all about what you are going through! Think about that. He knows! He knew about them because He was with them every step of the way. That is the same reason He knows what you are going through! He is with you every step of the way, too. And as He blessed them in their work, can you not know He is blessing the work you are doing out of love? He's watching every act of care with tenderness.

When my children were born I watched them breathe. I watched them sleep. I watched everything they did. They were my own, my babies, my precious ones. We are that to our Father God. We are never out of His sight and we are never out of His care and love. Rest in that, dear child of God.

Another bit of encouragement we can get from this passage is that the "trudge" will eventually come to an end. We will move through the great wilderness and into the Promised Land of victory He has chosen for us. Take courage!

**7 I will be glad and rejoice in your love, for you saw my
affliction and knew the anguish of my soul. Ps 31:7**

Prayer

How can I express my thanks, dear Father, for your tender watching over me? My wilderness is vast and my strength is small, but when I remember that you are here and you know my struggle it helps! It gives me hope and courage to trudge on. This is the path you have ordained for me and you will carry me through. I would not make it if that were not true. In grateful trust. Amen

How do you see God using these verses and these thoughts in your life today?

PROMISES FOR SLEEPLESS NIGHTS

**I will lie down and sleep in peace, for you alone,
O LORD, make me dwell in safety. Ps 4:8**

**I lie down and sleep; I wake again, because
the LORD sustains me. Ps 3:5**

Some years ago my husband needed to be gone for several nights. Of course this wasn't the first time for that, but this time was different. My children were no longer at home either. I would be spending my first night in the house all by myself! Now I was no child and as silly as it might seem, I was filled with dread. My great concern was that I would be awake all night, fearfully listening to all the sounds and imagining the worst. I began to pray for grace, strength and good sleep.

That morning I dropped him off at the airport just before 6:00 and as I started for home I turned on the radio to the Christian station. They were just beginning their daily broadcast and I could hardly believe what I was hearing! The announcer began with the verse of the day, one with which I was totally unfamiliar. It was Psalms 4:8. **"In peace I will both lie down and sleep, for you alone, O LORD, make me dwell in safety."**

The verse spoke healing to my fears immediately, but greater than the words were God's precious timing. I felt His grace surge through me as I knew He cared about even my sleep. I have quoted this verse to myself many nights since then and it has almost always brought me sleep, and it never fails to give me calm and peace as I remember how faithfully He answered the simple need of one of His fearful children.

I share this with you, dear one, because I know nights can be long and sleepless when grief, pressures and uncertainty surround us. These verses remind us that He does want us to have His rest. Commit them to memory and say them during those dark hours when it seems the rest of the world is sleeping. Don't be surprised to find yourself suddenly waking up to a new day refreshed! At the very least I believe you will find the peace and calm of your loving Father soothing your aching heart with peace and calm. Here are two more promises – He really means it!

When you lie down, you will not be afraid; when you lie down, your sleep will be sweet. Prov 3:24

...for he grants sleep to those he loves. Ps 127:2

Prayer

Father, the sleepless nights get long and scary. Can I really trust in these promises --that you will give me sleep? Days are so much easier to face when sleep has come. If you will help me, I will give you my burden, even if it is just for the night. How precious to know you really do care, and I am so grateful. Amen

How do you see God using these verses and these thoughts in your life today?

SAFE IN HIS HANDS

15 "Can a mother forget the baby at her breast
and have no compassion on the child she has borne?
Though she may forget,
I will not forget you!
16 See, I have engraved you on the palms of my hands;
your walls are ever before me. Isa 49:15-16

Engraved on God's hand! Some translations say, "tattooed" and perhaps that is a more descriptive picture in an age when tattoos are so popular. Kids everywhere are getting tattooed, so ask one of them, "Did it hurt?"

They will surely say "Yes, but it was worth it."

That's how it is for God, too. It cost Him great pain to engrave you on the palm of His hand, but He did it joyfully. It was worth it to Him! And once there, you cannot fall off, wash off, or wear off. When you come to Jesus your name is written indelibly in his Book of Life and your face is tattooed forever on His hand. May that thought sustain you in these hard times. You cannot fall from the Hand that is holding you up!

"Let the beloved of the LORD rest secure in him,
for he shields him all day long, Deut 33:12

Prayer

There are no words to tell you, Father, how much it means to me to rest in the security of your hands. Sometimes I forget how safe I really am and I get scared and lonely. But in those times, O Lord, remind me that my name, my very self, is securely engraved on your hand and I can never fall off. Thank you, thank, you, my blessed Place of Peace. Amen

How do you see God using these verses and these thoughts in your life today?

WHEN GOD SAYS NO

2 Cor 12:8-9 Three times I pleaded with the Lord to take it away from me. 9 But he said to me, "My grace is sufficient for you, for my power is made perfect in weakness." Therefore I will boast all the more gladly about my weaknesses, so that Christ's power may rest on me.

Has God answered "No" to your prayers? Well, you are in good company. Look at three men -- men who were deeply loved by God -- whose prayers were answered with a firm "No!" They were Moses, Paul, and Jesus.

In the above verses we see where Paul asked God to take away his illness and we see God's answer. It was no! Moses led God's people out of Egypt to the promised land of Canaan, but after all that effort, though Moses asked, God would not let him enter the land. "…**That is enough," the LORD said. "Do not speak to me anymore about this matter. 27 Go up to the top of Pisgah and look west and north and south and east. Look at the land with your own eyes, since you are not going to cross this Jordan. Deut. 3:26**

Jesus was God's own son and He prayed that the cup of suffering could be taken from Him. In each case God said "No!" to their requests, but in each case He answered with something profoundly more wonderful! Moses did not enter the earthly Promised Land, but was taken to the eternal Promised Land to be with the Lord forever. Paul found God's strength and grace in mighty measure. How wonderful to absolutely know that God is sufficient!

God said "No!" to Jesus, too. He had to "drink the cup" that God had called Him to, but the ultimate result of that suffering was the opening of heaven to all who would believe. Several verses point out that it was worth it to Jesus in the end.

After the suffering of his soul, he will see the light [of life] and be satisfied; by his knowledge my righteous servant will justify many, and he will bear their iniquities. Isa 53:11

Let us fix our eyes on Jesus, the author and perfecter of our faith, who for the joy set before him endured the cross, Heb 12:2

The Bible is clear about how much God loves each of us even as He loved Jesus, Paul and Moses. What this says to me is that when God says, "No!" to our prayers, then because of His love and faithfulness, we can expect that He has something far better down the road for us. We must keep our eyes on Him and wait with faith and hope! And we can know we are in good company!

Ps 27:13-14 I am still confident of this: I will see the goodness of the LORD in the land of the living. Wait for the LORD; be strong and take heart and wait for the LORD.

Prayer

Father, it is hard to take no for an answer when I care so deeply. You have said your grace is sufficient so I ask you now for the grace to accept whatever your answer is going to be. Help me to see your goodness through my tears and to find your peace as I wait. With trembling but trusting heart I ask in Jesus' name. Amen

How do you see God using these verses and these thoughts in your life today?

GOD, DO YOU REALLY KNOW MY PAIN?

You number my wanderings; Put my tears into Your bottle; Are they not in Your book? Ps 56:8-

the LORD will watch over your coming and going both now and forevermore. Ps 121:8

When I was young my bike skidded on gravel and sent me flying. I really messed up my knee. Almost immediately my mom was there to take me home and nurse me till I was back on my feet again. She always looked after me but ever so much more during those recovery days. I believe God is like that. His Father's heart is especially tender and caring when we are hurting. But when we gaze out at millions of stars, or contemplate the number of people on this planet, or consider the unimaginable varieties of living species it is easy to wonder, "How can God even know me, let alone be aware of what I am going through?"

The incredible beauty of God is that He understood that we would wonder. That's why He told us about His infinite care for us. He puts our tears in His bottle, He watches over our comings and goings, and Psalm 139 tells us He even knows what we are going to say before we say it. That's His Father's care for His precious children. And so, dear one, believe what He tells you. You are His own and He knows and cares about you. He doesn't stop there. These are His next promises:

…weeping may remain for a night, but rejoicing comes in the morning. Ps 30:5

Those who sow in tears will reap with songs of joy. Ps 126:5

Prayer

Dearest Father, it is so difficult for me to imagine that you are intimately involved in my struggle, and yet I have your word on it. Would you help me to absorb those promises into the depths of my soul so that I may feel your very hand wiping away my tears and comforting my aching heart? And even more wonderful, thank you for the promise that you will someday restore my joy. I am so grateful to you for being my place of hope and rest and expectation of joy. Amen

How do you see God using these verses and these thoughts in your life today?

OVERWHELMED!

Isa 43:1-2 "Fear not, for I have redeemed you; I have summoned you by name; you are mine. 2 When you pass through the waters, I will be with you; and when you pass through the rivers, they will not sweep over you. When you walk through the fire, you will not be burned;

When we are overwhelmed by the floods or the flames of life this verse is a little hard to believe! But amazingly we see in the book of Daniel that this promise was kept literally when the three young Hebrews walked out of the fiery furnace without a hair on their heads singed and they didn't even smell like smoke. They were told to worship a golden image or be thrown in the fire. They refused to bow down to anything but God and in great faith they told the king that God was able to save them. Look at their attitude of trust! , **"O Nebuchadnezzar, we do not need to defend ourselves before you in this matter. 17 If we are thrown into the blazing furnace, the God we serve is able to save us from it, and he will rescue us from your hand, O king. 18 But even if he does not, we want you to know, O king, that we will not serve your gods or worship the image of gold you have set up."**

They were completely sold out to God. Remember, these young men had been captured by an enemy king while they were in their early teens, taken away from their parents to a foreign country and forced to serve that king. Still, in all that pain, they trusted their Lord. Total relinquishment! Total trust! But how about me, how about you? That is one of the most difficult prayers to pray, and it usually comes when there is no alternative. I have been there, and God walked me through the flood. When I was told I had cancer I struggled so much -- the torrent started to overflow me. Then I said from my whole heart, "Lord, I cannot handle this! I have committed my life to you so whether I live or die, you are my God. I trust you."

There are not words to express the peace that flowed over me and carried me through the whole experience. And yet the circumstances never changed. There had been no mistake in the biopsy. God is bigger than anything that we are going through, and when that becomes absolute truth to us then even when they rise, the mighty waters will not reach

us! This is how the Hebrew children responded --total relinquishment to an all wise God who is utterly able and totally loving!

... we went through fire and water, but you brought us to a place of abundance. Ps 66:8-12

Therefore let everyone who is godly pray to you while you may be found; surely when the mighty waters rise, they will not reach him. Ps 32:6

Prayer

Oh, my Father. I feel like I am drowning and surrounded by flames. I am waiting for your promise to show yourself as my rescuer. Help me to look past the pain of my life into your loving face and trust that you're still on the throne and I am still on your heart. I cannot make it without you. So whatever you have for me I accept -- just give me the grace to get through the flood to your place of rest and safety. In desperation and hope. Amen.

How do you see God using these verses and these thoughts in your life today?

YOUR HOLY PURPOSE

"Yet who knows whether you have come to the kingdom for such a time as this?" Esther 4:14 (NKJV)

Queen Esther was a Jewish woman who became queen of Persia. In 474 B.C. she became the absolute only person in a position to save the Jews in that land from extinction. A huge responsibility rested on her delicate shoulders. The cousin who raised her laid this opportunity before her. **"Go to the king, your husband, and ask him to spare us or we will all die."** She might save her own life if she didn't go, because no one knew she was Jewish, but then her people would all die. On the other hand, if she went to him and he didn't want to see her, she might well be put to death immediately! Everything was on her shoulders.

Do you sometimes feel that way? It's all up to me! No one else can help! This is not a fun place to be. The verse tells us that Esther was hand-picked for this job at this time. This was her ordained purpose. We all have them, you know. Here are a few examples:

His words to Jeremiah: **"...Before I formed you in the womb I knew you; Before you were born I sanctified you; ..."** Jer 1:5

His words to us: **" It was he who gave some to be apostles, some to be prophets, some to be evangelists, and some to be pastors and teachers,"** Eph 4:11

His words to Pharaoh, showing He has purposes even for His enemies! **"I raised you up for this very purpose, that I might display my power in you and that my name might be proclaimed in all the earth." Rom 9:17**

We can see right away that some, even many, purposes are pretty challenging. So what is your ordained purpose? It mightn't be as dramatic as were Queen Esther's and Jeremiah's, but as Paul teaches we are all part of a body and though some are "noses" and some are "ears", we are ALL a necessary part. Your part is all on your shoulders! Perhaps your purpose right now is exactly what you are doing, caring for a loved one who needs you desperately. Perhaps it is to encourage others around you. But, dear one, your purpose is vital and you are just where you need to be. God is pleased with how you are serving His purpose, so be gracious to yourself. It's not an easy path and it may even be a long

and tedious road but you have risen to your call. Queen Esther, much like you, had to forget about herself, take up her cross and tackle her purpose. She saved the day for her people and you are saving the day for your loved one. Bless you, dear child of God.

The man who plants and the man who waters have one purpose, and each will be rewarded according to his own labor. 9 For we are God's fellow workers; 1 Cor 3:8-9

The LORD will fulfill [his purpose] for me; Ps 138:8

Prayer

Dear Lord, it is amazing that you, our almighty and majestic God, should be so intimately involved in my life that you would design a vital purpose just for me. Thank you for the trust you have in me. However, unless you do it all through me, I will fail. It is too big. Yet, here you promise to fulfill it and even reward it. Oh what desperately needed promises. I am eternally grateful. May I fulfill my purpose with grace. I love you, my precious Father. Amen

How do you see God using these verses and these thoughts in your life today?

STABILITY

**…and he will be the stability of your times, abundance
of salvation, wisdom and knowledge; Isaiah 33:6**

Have you ever been in an earthquake? I have only experienced minor tremors, but even in those everything trembles. There is nothing steady on which to hold and that makes it a fearful thing! Sometimes life hands us emotional "earthquakes". Everything we have grasped for security in the past fails us. Perhaps the one we have always leaned on is leaning now on us, or the trusted foundations of health or finances or family suddenly aren't there anymore. When life's foundations fall apart we surely feel like everything is out of control.

The good news, actually the great news, is that there is one Foundation that never gets shaken. God has promised to be the stability of our times, our steady rock that never fails.

**"See, I lay a stone in Zion, a tested stone, a precious
cornerstone for a sure foundation; the one who
trusts will never be dismayed. Isa 28:16**

God tells us in His Word that Jesus is our sure foundation! When we trust Him we will never be dismayed. He is the stability of our times, no matter how our world is trembling. He is there and He is enough!

**God is our refuge and strength, an ever-present help in trouble.
2 Therefore we will not fear, though the earth give way and the
mountains fall into the heart of the sea, 3 though its waters roar
and foam and the mountains quake with their surging. Ps 46:1-3**

**3 When the earth and all its people quake, it
is I who hold its pillars firm. Ps 75:3**

Prayer

Precious Lord Jesus, my Rock, my Foundation, my Stability, it feels sometimes as though I can't go on. Everything I have known in my life is shaking out of control. You alone remain steady. Help me, my Lord, to hold on to you with my last bit of strength and remind me of your promise to be the stability of my times. In the strong name of Jesus. Amen.

How do you see God using these verses and these thoughts in your life today?

HOW IN THE WORLD CAN
THIS WORK FOR GOOD?

8 Then the LORD said to Satan, "Have you considered my servant Job? There is no one on earth like him; he is blameless and upright, a man who fears God and shuns evil." Job 1:8

Why? It seems to be the first question that comes to our minds when suffering hits us. Of course we want to know -- we deserve an explanation! We think if we understand why then it will be easier to deal with. That may or may not be true, but as I look at the creativity of God seen in His varieties of insects, flowers and people it seems to me that there might also be an infinite number of reasons for the unique experiences of pain that God allows or ordains for us, each carefully allowed for exactly the right purposes. One of the most meaningful purposes for suffering I have observed, which I now believe is one of the universal reasons He allows it for His dear ones, is found in the first verses of the book of Job. We are told of Job in the very first verse that he was a blameless and upright man who feared God and shunned evil.

Job seems to be everything we believers try to be. Yet in all of Scripture no one except the Lord Jesus suffered as he did. But did you notice God's conversation with Satan? He is pointing out what a good man Job is. Satan went on to taunt that Job was good only because his life was so perfect, and anyone could be faithful under those circumstances! So God gave Satan permission to test this man. It was not a test to make him fall but to prove his strength!

God allowed the suffering of Job to prove to those who were watching, (Satan, we know, and I believe all the angels of heaven as well, along with each of us who read his story in the Bible) the faithfulness of one of God's people. I also believe there may be many watching us today during our difficult times -- the Father, the angels, and all who know us here on this earth. We can use any struggle life throws our way as a chance to exhibit the strength God gives to His children and testify that God is able to sustain His own!.

This makes me wonder -- does God trust the most those saints He allows to carry the heaviest loads? May our faithfulness in pain reveal the mighty power and grace of our God to a world that desperately

needs to see Him. And may that single purpose for our suffering give us strength to hold on!

One other happy note we learn from this passage. Suffering does not mean God is punishing us for sin. Job was blameless!

Prayer

Dear Lord, It is so difficult to live through hard times. Yet your Word tells me you are sovereign over every detail of my life. I want so much to be a witness for you, and you have trusted me to do that, but O my Father, you must be the One to do it through me. Without you I can do nothing, but in Christ I can do all things. In Him. Amen

How do you see God using these verses and these thoughts in your life today?

STRENGTH FOR YOUR DAYS

...and as your days, so shall your strength be. Deut. 33:25

My treasured friend is a double caregiver. Her mother is very frail and needy at 98 years old and her husband has two types of leukemia which are no longer in remission. Yesterday she hit the wall. She broke. She cried, her stomach burned and she couldn't eat. Have you ever been there? Are you there now?

It wrenched my heart. What could I do for her? I listened, I took her flowers and I prayed, but nothing seemed to change. It was a helpless feeling to realize this was her unique walk -- I couldn't change it. All I could do was support her through it. Then I was reminded once again of the faithfulness of our God. He *could* be there, *would* be there, every step of the way. He promised! [**I will never fail you or forsake you! Heb. 13:5**]

She was a little better the next day. She made it through another night. Doesn't seem like much of a victory -- or does it? Isaiah tell us,

" He gives strength to the weary and increases the power of the weak. 30 Even youths grow tired and weary, and young men stumble and fall; 31 but those who hope in the LORD will renew their strength. They will soar on wings like eagles; they will run and not grow weary, they will walk and not be faint." [Isa 40:29-31]

Sometimes just walking without fainting is a victory. And God has promised strength for each day, day after day, as long as we shall live. Her road may get harder before it gets easier, but He will never fail to carry her (or us) through. He has given His word. **As your days, so shall be your strength**! What a promise!

Prayer

Father, I pray for my friend, and for all your children who are burdened to the breaking point with the vital caring for their precious ones. It is such a mission, such a service, and such a ministry of love. But, dear Lord, it is so heavy. You know that. And you have promised to bring them through --- maybe not unscarred, but still intact. And how you cherish those earthly angels who are standing in for you in the lives of their needy ones. Thank you for the promise of strength for their days. In grateful praise. Amen.

How do you see God using these verses and these thoughts in your life today?

DECISIONS! TOO MANY TO COUNT

5 If any of you lacks wisdom, he should ask God, who gives generously to all without finding fault, and it will be given to him. 6 But when he asks, he must believe and not doubt, because he who doubts is like a wave of the sea, blown and tossed by the wind. James 1:5-6

It is so sad to be in a position of caring for a loved one and being reminded moment by moment of their weakness and need. Then, too, there is the heaviness of daily care and serving of that loved one. It surely seems unfair to add to that burden the very practical issues that must be dealt with, the decisions and daily challenges: the doctors, the utilities, the errands, the laundry, the shopping, the cooking, the insurance claims or premiums, the bank statement, the home maintenance, ad infinitum. Yet these must be done and done most likely without help from any one else. The whole thing rests again on you! "God, are you big enough to help me through this too," we may be asking.

Scripture once more is filled with messages from God that help us. We are told to ask for wisdom, and He will give it, but we must believe when we ask that we will receive that wisdom. That's hard! But, friend, if God knows everything, has perfect power and loves me totally (and I believe that on the authority of His word), then He can do it. And, if perhaps I miss His direction, or don't hear His voice as clearly as I ought, can I not trust Him to take care of the consequences? He tells us to ask and believe and then comes trust, trust for the results. Not trust in ourselves but trust in Him. Someone has said "God is totally prepared to take full responsibility for the person who is truly sold out to Him." Ours is just to seek His face and trust His grace --- His is to be faithful. After all, He is God! Some more verses:

My son, if you accept my words and store up my commands within you, 2 turning your ear to wisdom and applying your heart to understanding, 3 and if you call out for insight and cry aloud for understanding, 4 and if you look for it as for silver and search for it as for hidden treasure, 5 then you will understand the fear of the LORD and find the knowledge

of God. 6 For the LORD gives wisdom, and from his
mouth come knowledge and understanding. Prov 2:1-6

5 Trust in the LORD with all your heart and lean not on
your own understanding; 6 in all your ways acknowledge
him, and he will make your paths straight. Prov 3:5-6

Prayer

*Dear Father, Source of all wisdom. I am often so confused and burdened
down with the little decisions and daily practical demands that sometimes
these things loom larger than even the care of my dear one. That ought not
to be. But I am only human and all I can do is all I can do. I throw myself
on your mercy now. Will you, I plead, give me answers, wisdom, direction,
guidance for these issues that scream at me day after day, so that I may be
about the good business of loving my loved one calmly? With gratitude and
hope, in the name of my Savior. Amen*

How do you see God using these verses and these thoughts in your life today?

THE POWER OF THE WORD

10 As the rain and the snow come down from heaven, and do not return to it without watering the earth and making it bud and flourish, so that it yields seed for the sower and bread for the eater, 11 so is my word that goes out from my mouth: It will not return to me empty, but will accomplish what I desire and achieve the purpose for which I sent it. Isa 55:10-11

"Take time to read the Bible? Are you kidding? I can hardly get through every day as it is -- I can't afford the luxury of reading the paper, let alone study the Bible (although I know I should)." You might be thinking that and I understand, dear one. The days are long, the tasks are many and the energy is low. Yet just look at the promise of our Father, the One who made us and knows us better than we know ourselves. He says His word never goes out without bearing the fruit that He intended it to bear. That means every time I open my Bible He is up to something in my life. What a promise, and what an incentive!

Look at Jesus when He was tempted in the wilderness. (Matt. 4) The weapon He used to stand strong was the Word of God. With every temptation His resistance was based on truth from God's written word. And it was the strength He needed! Paul described the protective spiritual armor we need in Ephesians 6 and the only offensive weapon he gave us was **" the sword of the Spirit, which is the word of God." Eph 6:17-18**

Beloved, that's why these devotions are so full of Scripture. The words of this author are humble attempts at encouragement from one human heart to another, but the Bible carries the words of the Author of life itself and He has the answers for all our needs. Turn to Him; turn to His words and find healing and encouragement. He loves you so! Read these several more affirmations of His word.

2 Let my teaching fall like rain and my words descend like dew, like showers on new grass, like abundant rain on tender plants. Deut 32:2

35 Heaven and earth will pass away, but my words will never pass away. Matt 24:35

63 The Spirit gives life; the flesh counts for nothing. The words I have spoken to you are spirit and they are life. John 6:62-64

Prayer

Dear God, Giver of life and Author of the Words that sustain us, I ask you now to give me the grace and discipline to spend even a few minutes each day in your Bible. Will you quicken the truth I find there to my heart and use it to accomplish just what you purpose for me? Some days I may need peace, some days wisdom and some days comfort or strength. But you, oh Holy Creator, know best what I need to find in the pages of your "love letter" to me. May I do my part. In the name of the Living Word. Amen

How do you see God using these verses and these thoughts in your life today?

LORD, I MISS "NORMAL"

2 How long, O LORD, must I call for help, but you do not listen? Hab 1:2

I asked my friend who has cared for her severely handicapped daughter for over a dozen years what she has found the most difficult. Without hesitation she replied, "I miss "normal".

I can imagine that is true of countless caregivers of every age. Thoughts like; "Will life ever be normal again?" "Lord, I really do miss normal!" In a normal world my challenged child would be going out for a play date instead of going to be fitted for a new wheel chair! My spouse and I would be joining friends for an evening out, perhaps dinner and a movie. If life were normal, I would be spending my afternoons in the garden instead of at the nursing home with my aged mother." Are these the thoughts you are having, dear one? What *is* normal about your life are these thoughts! Even Habakkuk, one of God's prophets, questioned God. "How long until you hear me, Lord?" Don't we ask the same question?

One of the most difficult thought processes is the one that fantasizes on "what might have been." God is a God of this day and this situation. No person can really answer the "whys" of this life but God has promised in Hebrews 13:5

"…Never will I leave you; never will I forsake you." Heb. 13:5

And in Jeremiah: **11 For I know the plans I have for you," declares the LORD, "plans to prosper you and not to harm you, plans to give you hope and a future. Jer 29:11**

And He adds in Romans this thought: **28 And we know that in all things God works for the good of those who love him, who have been called according to his purpose. Rom 8:28**

We cannot imagine how these promises can be true when we are bogged down in why's and yearnings for normalcy. I believe for God's children there is no "normal" He has gone before us and knows all our ways. We are unique in our very selves and in whatever circumstances He has ordained or allowed for us. Our best recourse is acceptance with hope, which is how Habakkuk ended his questioning of God.

17 Though the fig tree does not bud and there are no grapes on the vines, though the olive crop fails and the fields produce no food, though there are no sheep in the pen and no cattle in the stalls, 18 yet I will rejoice in the LORD, I will be joyful in God my Savior. 19 The Sovereign LORD is my strength; he makes my feet like the feet of a deer, he enables me to go the heights. Hab 3:17-19

Prayer

Oh, my Father, how I long for the seemingly normal lives others are leading: children who play, spouses who dance, parents who respond, but that is not where you have me. My plea is that you will give me the grace to accept my path and trust that you are leading me and my beloved ultimately to a good place. In hope and shaky trust. Amen.

How do you see God using these verses and these thoughts in your life today?

YOU ARE LOVED

**17 But from everlasting to everlasting the LORD's
love is with those who fear him, Ps 103:17**

**"I have loved you with an everlasting love; I have
drawn you with loving-kindness. 4 I will build you
up again and you will be rebuilt, Jer 31:3-4**

I can't even remember the circumstances. All I remember is being in my room -- a small child feeling very unloved. I probably had just received a scolding for something, and most likely my feelings were combined with guilt. Whatever the situation, I was downhearted and feeling alone. I do remember clearly that I wrote a note to my mother saying, "I'm sorry you don't love me anymore," and laid it on the end of the ironing board where she was working. I ran to sulk after that and was surprised by a huge feeling of remorse. There was no question my mother loved me! She told me and showed me countless times a day. In panic I ran back to retrieve my note before she could read it and, gratefully, it was in the same place, seemingly untouched.

As an adult I can speculate that she read it, wisely anticipated my remorse and replaced it quickly. She knew I would soon realize she adored me and would be ashamed of my doubts. As this memory lingers I can transfer it to God's love. When things go badly and times are difficult there is a tendency to not only ask, "God, where are you?" but also to question, "Do you really love me?" His word is clear. He loves us with an everlasting love, even when we may not have pleased Him. Though we may have doubted Him, like my mother He trusts we will soon discover that, "everlasting" still means forever. Jesus, speaking the Father's words always, reinforced this truth.

**9 "As the Father has loved me, so have I loved
you. Now remain in my love. John 15:9**

It appears from Scripture that the question is settled. May it be settled always in your mind, even in your down days --- God loves you! One more scriptural reminder:

**Give thanks to the LORD, for he is good;
his love endures forever. Ps 118:1**

Prayer

My loving Father, how sweet and comforting it is to know that you really are my loving Father! Sometimes I forget. Sometimes I have trouble believing it. But you have said it, so I will claim it. I need desperately to know your love when I feel so alone and unloved. Thank you, God, that those feelings are simply untrue. By your grace I will continue to lean on you. Amen.

How do you see God using these verses and these thoughts in your life today?

DEATH, THE LAST ENEMY

"Jesus wept" John 11:35 .

The actress Bette Davis in her latter years has been credited with saying that old age is not for sissies. I am seeing the truth of that more and more each day as the years pile on. One of the hardest things about getting older is watching beloved friends struggle with illness and death, their own or that of a family member. Paul called death the last enemy to be defeated, [1 Cor 15:26] and he is indeed a formidable foe, but dear one, he is a mortally wounded enemy, a toothless tiger, since our dear Lord Jesus defeated him on Calvary!

The shortest verse in the Bible (but one of the sweetest!) is "Jesus wept." He wept at the tomb of Lazarus. He knew He was going to raise Lazarus from the dead, so why did He weep? I believe He was thinking of each one of us and was identifying with the grief we would face when we lost our loved ones. Perhaps it was this very identification that helped Him walk His precious redeeming trek up Calvary's mountain. Just a few verses earlier in this chapter Jesus made perhaps the greatest promise of His life.

"Jesus said to her, "I am the resurrection and the life. He who believes in me will live, even though he dies; 26 and whoever lives and believes in me will never die." John 11:25-26

Then, I believe, because we cannot see the other side when our loved ones dance for joy in the presence of the Holy One, He gave us a visual example of resurrection. Lazarus walked out of the tomb. Those around saw it clearly and we can read the story and picture the scene. Therefore we can know that's what happens at the moment of death for God's children. They rise to new life with great joy!

He felt our pain, He gave us His promise, and He showed us what resurrection looked like, and then He poured out His life's blood to make it happen. We can hang on to that and rejoice that we do not have to **"grieve as those who have no hope."**

13 Brothers, we do not want you to be ignorant

**about those who fall asleep, or to grieve like the
rest of men, who have no hope. 1 Thess 4:13**

Prayer

Dear Jesus, the final enemy is still such an agonizing part of our lives. How comforting it is to know that you weep with us when we grieve. It's even better to realize that death has been defeated by your cross -- that we are able to claim the promise that because of you, when death comes for a believer he just crosses over into eternal life. We grieve at the temporary loss but rejoice in the hope that comes only from you. We cannot adequately express our gratitude, dear Redeemer and friend. Amen